BREAKING THE CYCLE:

A Comprehensive Guide to Conquering Pornography Addiction

Rodrigo Ciaralo

TABLE OF CONTENTS

- The brain's neuroplasticity allows for "reprogramming" through therapy.
- Neuroimaging studies reveal alterations in brain areas associated with reward, emotions, and decision-making.

Chapter 4: Risk Factors and Vulnerabilities

- Genetic factors can influence reward sensitivity, dopamine regulation, and impulsivity.
- Psychological factors like low self-esteem, social anxiety, depression, and mental disorders can increase vulnerability.
- Environmental factors include early exposure, social norms, and easy access to pornography.
- Adverse life experiences can contribute to addiction.

Chapter 5: Consequences of Pornography Addiction

- Physical consequences include erectile dysfunction, premature or delayed ejaculation, genital pain, and exhaustion.
- Psychological consequences include anxiety, depression, low self-esteem, social isolation, concentration difficulties, and distorted body image.
- Social consequences involve intimacy problems, marital conflicts, and isolation from family and friends.
- Social and professional consequences include decreased productivity and difficulty maintaining employment.

Chapter 6: Unraveling Cognitive Behavioral Therapy (CBT)

- CBT is a powerful approach to recover from pornography addiction.
- CBT is based on the idea that thoughts, emotions, and behaviors are interconnected.
- CBT aims to identify and modify thoughts and behaviors that sustain addiction.
- CBT utilizes neuroplasticity to "reprogram" the brain.

Chapter 7: CBT Techniques in Practice

- Identifying triggers involves recognizing external and internal cues that lead to consumption.

- Cognitive restructuring challenges and modifies distorted thoughts.
- Relapse prevention involves developing a plan to avoid high-risk situations.
- Emotional regulation techniques help manage negative emotions.
- Exposure and response prevention (ERP) involves gradual exposure to triggers without engaging in compulsive behavior.

Chapter 8: Adapting CBT

- CBT can be adapted to different populations, including adolescents, couples, and individuals with coexisting mental disorders.
- Adolescent treatment requires shorter sessions, dynamic activities, and family involvement.
- Couples therapy rebuilds intimacy, trust, and communication.
- Individuals with comorbidities require an integrated approach to address all aspects of mental health.

Chapter 9: The Strength of Evidence

- CBT has been shown to reduce consumption, minimize compulsive behaviors, alleviate cravings, and improve psychological well-being.
- Meta-analyses support the effectiveness of CBT for behavioral addictions.
- Research suggests CBT affects brain areas related to executive control, emotional reactivity, and reward processing.
- Further research is needed to address gaps and enhance protocols.

Chapter 10: Integrating Approaches

- Integrating CBT with other therapies can enhance recovery.
- Couples therapy addresses relationship challenges and rebuilds intimacy.
- Pharmacotherapy can manage psychiatric comorbidities and neurochemical dysregulation.

- Mindfulness cultivates present-moment awareness and reduces reactivity.
- Acceptance and Commitment Therapy (ACT) aligns actions with personal values.

Chapter 11: Diving into Psychoanalysis

- Psychoanalysis explores the unconscious motivations that fuel addiction.
- It examines unconscious conflicts, fixation in developmental stages, and compulsive repetition.
- Psychoanalytic treatment aims to bring unconscious conflicts to light and work through them.

Chapter 12: Preventing Pornography Addiction

- Prevention requires a collective effort from governments, schools, families, and communities.
- Comprehensive sexual education is crucial, covering healthy relationships, media literacy, and risks of excessive consumption.
- Developing socioemotional skills like self-esteem, assertiveness, and emotional regulation is essential.
- Creating safe online and offline environments protects individuals from addiction.

Chapter 13: Ethical and Social Considerations

- The pornographic industry raises ethical concerns about exploitation, objectification, and hypersexualization of culture.
- Individuals have the responsibility to consume consciously and seek help for addiction.
- Collective responsibility involves education, industry regulation, and public policies promoting mental health.

Chapter 14: Behind the Camera

- The pornographic industry perpetuates myths about its harmlessness, the well-being of actors, and realistic sexuality.
- The industry faces issues like human trafficking, sexual abuse, financial exploitation, and mental health problems among actors.

- Consumers can choose ethical productions, support organizations fighting exploitation, and promote comprehensive sexual education.

Chapter 15: Decades of Exposure to Pornography

- Prolonged exposure to pornography can affect the brain's reward system, increase sensitization, reduce gray matter, and impact relationships.
- Research continues to explore the long-term effects and how to reverse them.

Chapter 16: Spirituality and Recovery

- Spirituality, the search for meaning and connection, can be an important factor in recovery.
- Spirituality promotes mental well-being, self-knowledge, and human connection.
- It helps individuals find purpose, develop self-awareness, and cultivate compassion.
- Spirituality can be integrated into treatment through meditation, group participation, and connection with nature.

Chapter 17: A Message of Hope

- Recovery from pornography addiction is possible.
- Individuals are encouraged to believe in their ability to change, seek support, and find strength in themselves and others.
- Spirituality, purpose, and self-compassion are emphasized on the recovery journey.

Conclusion

- Pornography addiction is a complex issue with individual, social, and ethical dimensions.
- The path forward involves investing in education, expanding support services, promoting research, holding the industry accountable, using technology consciously, and fostering dialogue.
- A collective effort is needed to build a society where sexuality is experienced fully, healthily, and consciously.

Conclusion

INTRODUCTION

Welcome to a Journey of Self-Knowledge and Transformation:

In an era dominated by the internet and the accessibility of pornography, pornography addiction has become a growing challenge, affecting the lives of millions of people worldwide. If you are reading this book, you are likely seeking answers, solutions, and a path to free yourself from the grips of addiction.

This book is a comprehensive guide to recovering from pornography addiction, based on scientific knowledge, tools from Cognitive Behavioral Therapy (CBT), and a human and compassionate approach.

Exploring the Labyrinth of Addiction:

Throughout this book, we will delve into the labyrinth of pornography addiction, exploring its causes, its consequences, and the paths to recovery. We will unravel the brain mechanisms that sustain addiction, understand the risk and vulnerability factors, and learn to use CBT tools to "reprogram" the brain and build a freer and more fulfilling life.

A Comprehensive and Individualized Approach:

This book offers a comprehensive and individualized approach to treating pornography addiction, recognizing that each person is unique and that addiction manifests differently in each individual. We will explore adaptations of CBT for adolescents, couples, and people with coexisting mental disorders, ensuring that each reader finds the tools and strategies best suited to their needs.

A Path of Hope and Transformation:

We believe that recovery from pornography addiction is possible and that this book can be a valuable guide on this journey. Throughout the chapters, we will share inspiring stories of people who have overcome addiction, offer practical exercises and reflections, and provide tips and strategies to deal with the challenges of recovery.

Together, We Will Build a Healthier and More Conscious Future:

In addition to individual treatment, we will address the ethical and social implications of pornography addiction, critically analyzing the pornographic industry and its impacts on culture, sexuality, and relationships. We will also discuss the importance of prevention and building a more ethical and just future, where sexuality is experienced with more freedom, responsibility, and respect.

We invite you to embark on this journey of self-knowledge and transformation, unraveling the mysteries of pornography addiction and walking the path of recovery. Together, we can build a healthier, more conscious future free from addiction.

CHAPTER 1

The History of Pornography: From Caves to the Digital Age

A Millennia-Long Journey:

Pornography, although often associated with the digital age and the internet, has a long and complex history that dates back to the dawn of civilization. It's as if pornography were a river flowing through the centuries, shaping culture, sexuality, and relationships over time.

In this chapter, we will embark on a fascinating journey through the history of pornography, exploring its origins, transformations, and impacts on society.

Ancient Origins:

The earliest manifestations of pornography can be found in cave paintings, sculptures, and art objects that depict erotic and sexual scenes. It's as if our ancestors were leaving secret messages on cave walls, expressing their desires and fantasies.

In ancient Greece and Rome, pornography was present in plays, poems, and works of art, reflecting the sexual freedom and fascination with the human body that characterized these cultures. It's as if pornography was a way to celebrate life and sexuality without the constraints of morality and repression.

The Era of Repression:

With the rise of Christianity and other monotheistic religions, sexuality began to be seen as something sinful and shameful, and pornography was condemned and censored. It's as if the river of pornography was dammed, its waters hidden under a veil of prohibitions and taboos.

During the Middle Ages and the Early Modern Period, pornography circulated clandestinely through books, pamphlets, and engravings. It's as if the river found underground paths to continue flowing despite the obstacles.

The Industrial Revolution and the Rise of Media:

The Industrial Revolution, with its technological innovations, boosted the production and distribution of pornography. Photography, cinema, and video opened new possibilities for the representation of sexuality, and pornography began to reach an increasingly larger audience. It's as if the river had broken its dam, flooding society with its waters.

In the 20th century, pornography became a multibillion-dollar industry, driven by sexual liberation and the popularization of

the internet. It's as if the river had transformed into an ocean, with waves reaching every corner of the planet.

The Digital Age: Pornography at the Click of a Button:

The internet revolutionized the way people consume pornography, making it accessible anytime and anywhere, just a click away. It's as if pornography were in the palm of our hand, available 24 hours a day.

This unprecedented accessibility brought new challenges, such as the increase in pornography addiction, the early exposure of children and adolescents to sexually explicit content, and the proliferation of violent and degrading material.

It's as if the ocean of pornography were being agitated by storms, with giant waves threatening people's safety and well-being.

The Future of Pornography:

The future of pornography is uncertain, but some trends indicate significant changes:

- **Virtual Reality and Artificial Intelligence:** Virtual reality and artificial intelligence promise to revolutionize the experience of pornography, creating immersive and personalized virtual worlds. It's as if pornography were creating new universes with infinite possibilities for exploration and experimentation.
- **Ethical and Feminist Productions:** The movement for more ethical and feminist pornography is growing, respecting human rights, gender equality, and diversity. It's as if new vessels are emerging in the ocean of pornography, navigating with responsibility and awareness.
- **Awareness and Regulation:** Awareness of the impacts of pornography and the need for industry regulation are increasing. It's as if society is building dams and lighthouses to control the flow of the ocean and ensure the safety of navigation.

Final Considerations:

Throughout its millennia-long history, pornography has been a reflection of the culture, sexuality, and values of each era. It's as if it were a mirror reflecting the image of society, with its lights and shadows.

Understanding the history of pornography allows us to critically analyze the present and build a more conscious and responsible future, where sexuality is experienced in a healthier and more fulfilling way.

CHAPTER 2

Definitions: Pornography Addiction in Perspective

The Ubiquity of Pornography in the Digital Age

In the digital age, pornography has become an omnipresent phenomenon, accessible to anyone with an internet connection, regardless of age, gender, or culture. This unprecedented accessibility has brought with it a series of challenges, including the increase in the number of people struggling with pornography addiction.

Imagine the internet as a vast ocean of information, where pornography is a strong and seductive current. For many, navigating this current is a recreational and harmless experience, but for others, it can become a dangerous trap, leading to addiction and suffering.

Defining Pornography Addiction: A Complex Challenge

Precisely defining pornography addiction is a challenge that intrigues and divides the scientific community. Controversies arise from the complexity of human behavior and the lack of universal consensus on what constitutes an "addiction," especially when it involves behaviors rather than substances.

Unlike substance addictions, such as drugs or alcohol, which involve physical dependence and withdrawal symptoms, pornography addiction is classified as a behavioral addiction. In this case, dependence is predominantly psychological, manifesting in patterns of compulsive consumption and loss of control.

One of the most accepted definitions of pornography addiction describes a consumption pattern characterized by:

- **Loss of Control:** Inability to control the frequency, duration, and intensity of pornography consumption, even in the face of negative consequences. It's as if the individual is driving a car at high speed without brakes toward a cliff.
- **Compulsion:** A strong desire or irresistible urge to consume pornography, even when the person wants to stop. It's like an itch that doesn't stop, an urgent need that dominates thoughts and actions.
- **Neglect of Other Areas of Life:** Prioritizing pornography consumption over responsibilities, relationships, and important activities. It's as if life is a garden, but the person only dedicates themselves to watering a single plant, leaving the others to wither and die.
- **Negative Consequences:** Experiencing significant negative consequences, such as relationship problems, professional setbacks, sexual dysfunction, guilt, and shame. It's as if the person is building a sandcastle by the sea, ignoring the approaching tide that threatens to destroy everything.

Differentiating Pornography Addiction from Other Sexual Behaviors

It is crucial to distinguish pornography addiction from other healthy and pleasurable sexual behaviors. Human sexuality is rich and diverse, encompassing a broad spectrum of desires, fantasies, and behaviors. A healthy sexual behavior is characterized by:

- **Mutual Consent:** Respecting the will and boundaries of all involved individuals.
- **Shared Pleasure:** Seeking pleasurable and satisfying experiences for everyone involved.
- **Harmonious Integration into the Individual's Life:** Sexuality is a natural and integrated part of life, contributing to physical and emotional well-being without harming other areas.

Pornography addiction, on the other hand, is like a virus that infects and distorts sexuality, turning it into a source of suffering and conflict. Compulsion, loss of control, and negative consequences mark this experience, harming the individual's life and that of their loved ones.

Diagnostic Controversies: DSM-5 and ICD-11

The lack of universal consensus on pornography addiction is reflected in the absence of a formal and specific diagnosis in the DSM-5 (Diagnostic and Statistical Manual of Mental Disorders) and the ICD-11 (International Classification of Diseases).

This absence of a formal diagnosis does not diminish the suffering and negative impacts of pornography addiction. It's as if the person is experiencing intense pain, but there is no name to describe that pain. However, the lack of a diagnosis highlights the need for more research to deepen the understanding of the problem and develop more precise diagnostic criteria.

Proposed Diagnostic Criteria for Research

Despite the lack of a formal diagnosis, various studies propose criteria to assess and classify pornography addiction, generally including:

- **Frequency and Duration of Consumption:** How much time the person spends consuming pornography and how frequently.
- **Attempts to Control:** Whether the person has unsuccessfully tried to reduce or control consumption.
- **Negative Consequences:** Negative impact of consumption on different areas of life (relationships, work, mental health, etc.).
- **Intense Desire (Craving):** Presence of uncontrollable urges for pornography.
- **Use Despite Consequences:** Continuing to consume pornography even when aware of the negative consequences.

Final Considerations

Understanding the complexity of pornography addiction is the first step toward recovery. Recognizing the signs, diagnostic controversies, and proposed research criteria paves the way for seeking help and beginning the journey toward a freer and fuller life.

In the following chapters, we will delve deeper into the neurobiological mechanisms of addiction, the tools of Cognitive Behavioral Therapy (CBT), and strategies to rebuild your life free from pornography addiction.

CHAPTER 3

**The Neuroscience of Pornography Addiction:
Unraveling the Reprogrammed Brain**

Delving into the Brain Labyrinth

Understanding pornography addiction, like any other addiction, requires a journey into the depths of our brain labyrinth. It is necessary to unravel the neurobiological mechanisms that sustain this compulsive behavior, understand how the brain is affected by excessive consumption, and how this perpetuates the vicious cycle of addiction.

Imagine the brain as a dense and complex forest, with trails and paths that intersect and interconnect. Pornography addiction is like a narrow and dark path that, with each step, becomes deeper and harder to exit. Neuroscience is the compass that will guide us through this forest, revealing the paths taken by addiction and helping us find the trail to recovery.

The Reward System: Pleasure at Stake

At the center of this brain forest lies the reward system, a complex and powerful neural network responsible for generating feelings of pleasure and reinforcing behaviors essential for survival, such as eating, drinking, and reproducing. It's as if the reward system were a lush garden where feelings of pleasure and well-being flourish.

Dopamine, a key neurotransmitter in this system, acts like fertilizer in this garden, nourishing feelings of pleasure and motivation. However, excessive consumption of pornography can lead to a dopamine overdose, overstimulating the reward system and creating an imbalance. It's as if too much fertilizer, instead of nurturing the garden, is suffocating it, preventing new flowers from growing.

The Trap of Dysregulation

With repeated exposure to intense and artificial sexual stimuli, the brain adapts, seeking a new balance. This adaptation leads to desensitization, meaning a decrease in the sensitivity of dopamine receptors. It's as if the reward system's garden has become accustomed to the fertilizer overdose, requiring increasingly larger doses to produce the same pleasure flowers.

This desensitization explains the difficulty in controlling pornography consumption, even in the face of negative consequences. The brain, seeking the pleasure that was once easily obtained, demands larger doses, leading to a vicious cycle of increased consumption and loss of control.

Neuroplasticity: The Ever-Changing Brain

The good news is that the brain possesses an incredible ability to remodel itself in response to new experiences, a phenomenon known as neuroplasticity. It's as if the brain forest is in constant transformation, with new trails and paths forming every moment.

This capacity for change is the foundation for recovering from pornography addiction. Through Cognitive Behavioral Therapy (CBT) and other therapeutic approaches, it is possible to "reprogram" the brain, creating new trails and paths that lead to healthier and more fulfilling behaviors.

Neuroimaging Studies: Mapping the Brain Forest

Neuroimaging studies, such as functional magnetic resonance imaging (fMRI), allow us to visualize the brain changes related to pornography addiction. It's as if we have a map of the brain forest, showing the areas affected by addiction and the paths taken by compulsion.

These studies reveal alterations in brain areas such as:

- **Nucleus Accumbens:** A region of the reward system that becomes hyperactive in response to pornographic stimuli, intensifying the sensation of pleasure and the desire to consume more.
- **Amygdala:** A brain region involved in processing emotions, which becomes hypersensitive in individuals with pornography addiction, increasing emotional reactivity and impulsivity.
- **Prefrontal Cortex:** The area responsible for inhibitory control, decision-making, and planning, which shows reduced activity in individuals with pornography addiction, making behavioral control more difficult.

Sensitization: The Path of Desire (Craving)

Another important mechanism is sensitization, a process that makes the reward system more sensitive to pornography-related stimuli. It's as if the path of desire becomes wider and deeper each time it's traveled, leading to more intense and frequent cravings.

These cravings, or uncontrollable urges, are one of the main obstacles in recovering from pornography addiction. It's as if the person is being pulled back to the dark path of addiction, even when they are trying to find the way to recovery.

Final Considerations: Finding the Way Out of the Forest

Neuroscience helps us understand how pornography addiction affects the brain, revealing the mechanisms that sustain this compulsive behavior. This understanding is fundamental for developing effective therapeutic interventions, such as Cognitive Behavioral Therapy (CBT), which we will explore in the following chapters.

Remember, pornography addiction is not a moral or character failure but a complex condition with neurobiological foundations. It's as if the person is lost in the forest, not knowing how to find the exit. CBT acts as an experienced guide, showing the way and providing the necessary tools for recovery.

CHAPTER 4

Risk Factors and Vulnerabilities for Pornography Addiction: Unraveling the Roots of the Problem

Pornography Addiction: A Web of Influences

Pornography addiction, like other behavioral addictions, does not arise by chance. It is like a seed finding fertile ground to germinate and grow, driven by a combination of risk factors and vulnerabilities.

Imagine a complex web, where each thread represents a factor that contributes to the development of addiction. Genetic, psychological, environmental factors, and life experiences intertwine, creating a network of influences that can lead to compulsive pornography consumption.

In this chapter, we will explore each of these threads, unraveling the roots of the problem and understanding how different factors can make a person more vulnerable to pornography addiction.

Genetic Factors: Inherited Predisposition

Although there is no "addiction gene," genetics play an important role in an individual's predisposition to developing addictive behaviors, including pornography addiction. It's as if some people inherit a more fertile soil for addiction development, while others inherit more resilient soil.

Genetic variations can influence how the reward system responds to pleasure, dopamine regulation, and impulsivity. It's as if some people have a more sensitive reward system, constantly seeking pleasurable stimuli, while others have a more balanced system.

Twin studies and genetic analyses have identified genes related to the dopaminergic system and impulse control that can increase the risk of addiction. It's as if genetics provide the map of the brain forest, with some paths more prone to leading to addiction than others.

Psychological Factors: Internal Vulnerabilities

Various psychological factors can make a person more vulnerable to pornography addiction. It's as if some people carry an emotional baggage that makes them more susceptible to seeking comfort and escape in addictive behaviors.

- **Low Self-Esteem:** People with low self-esteem may use pornography as a form of validation and escape from self-criticism. It's as if they seek in pornography a mirror that reflects a distorted and idealized image of themselves.
- **Social Anxiety:** Social anxiety can lead to seeking virtual social interactions, where pornography offers the illusion of connection without the risk of rejection. It's as if the person builds a wall around themselves, seeking refuge in a virtual world.
- **Depression:** Depression can lead to using pornography as a means of escape and relief from emotional pain. It's as if the person seeks in pornography a painkiller to numb the suffering.
- **Mental Disorders:** Disorders such as Obsessive-Compulsive Disorder (OCD) and Attention-Deficit/

Hyperactivity Disorder (ADHD) can increase impulsivity and difficulty in control, making the person more vulnerable to addiction. It's as if the brain is in a constant state of alert, seeking stimuli and distractions.

Environmental Factors: The Influence of the Surrounding World

The social and cultural environment we live in also exerts significant influence on the development of pornography addiction. It's as if the environment were the climate of the brain forest, influencing the growth and direction of the trails.

- **Early Exposure:** Early exposure to pornography, especially during adolescence, can shape a person's view of sex and relationships, making them more susceptible to addiction. It's as if the person is learning to ride a bicycle on a bumpy and dangerous road.
- **Social Norms:** The normalization of pornography consumption in certain social groups can influence individual attitudes and behaviors. It's as if the person is following a trail that everyone around them seems to be walking, without questioning if this is the right direction.
- **Accessibility:** The internet and mobile devices facilitate access to pornography, making it available anytime and anywhere. It's as if the person is carrying a map of the brain forest with the addiction trail always in sight.

Life Experiences: Traumas and Scars

Adverse life experiences, such as sexual abuse, neglect, domestic violence, and childhood traumas, can leave deep scars on the psyche, increasing vulnerability to pornography addiction. It's as if the person is carrying an open wound, seeking in pornography a bandage that only intensifies the pain.

Pornography can be used as a dysfunctional coping mechanism to deal with the emotional consequences of trauma. It's as if the person is trying to extinguish a fire with gasoline, worsening the situation.

Interaction of Factors: A Systemic Perspective

It is important to remember that pornography addiction is multifactorial, resulting from the complex interaction between genetics, psychology, environment, and life experiences. It's as if each thread of the web contributes to the formation of addiction, with different weights and intensities.

Understanding this interaction is crucial for developing more effective and personalized intervention and prevention strategies. It's as if we are weaving a new web, with stronger and healthier threads, that supports recovery and well-being.

CHAPTER 5

Consequences of Pornography Addiction: A Multifaceted Impact

Pornography addiction, like a whirlwind, drags along a series of consequences that spread across various areas of an individual's life, impacting physical health, psychological well-being, interpersonal relationships, and social and professional performance. It's like a stone thrown into a calm lake, creating waves that propagate and alter the surrounding landscape.

In this chapter, we will dive into the depths of these consequences, exploring how pornography addiction can affect every aspect of a person's life, from the most intimate relationships to the way they relate to themselves.

Physical Consequences: Beyond the Act

It is common to think that pornography addiction manifests only in the psychological realm, but its physical consequences are real and can be quite significant. Compulsive masturbation, often associated with addiction, can lead to:

- **Erectile Dysfunction:** Constant exposure to intense and artificial sexual stimuli from pornography can lead to desensitization, making it difficult to achieve and maintain an erection during sex with a real partner.

It's as if the body becomes accustomed to such a high "volume" of stimulation that real interactions lose the ability to generate excitement.

- **Premature or Delayed Ejaculation:** Pornography addiction can also affect ejaculation mechanisms, leading to premature ejaculation or, in some cases, delayed ejaculation or anorgasmia. It's as if the body loses the ability to regulate the natural rhythm of the sexual response, out of sync with the frequency and intensity of masturbation.
- **Genital Pain and Discomfort:** Frequent and vigorous masturbation can cause pain, irritation, and discomfort in the genital area, similar to a muscle being pushed beyond its limits and becoming injured.
- **Physical Exhaustion:** The vicious cycle of addiction, with the relentless pursuit of pornography and compulsive masturbation, can lead to physical exhaustion and a lack of energy. It's as if the body is in a constant state of alert, consuming energy without having time to recharge.

Psychological Consequences: An Invisible Burden

Pornography addiction carries with it a psychological burden that can be devastating, contributing to the development or worsening of various mental health issues:

- **Anxiety and Depression:** Pornography addiction is often associated with feelings of guilt, shame, anxiety, and depression. It's as if the person is carrying an invisible weight that prevents them from breathing freely and distances them from the joy of living.
- **Low Self-Esteem:** Constant comparison with unrealistic and idealized images in pornography can lead to dissatisfaction with one's own body and a decrease in self-esteem. It's as if the person looks in the mirror and only sees flaws, feeling inadequate and inferior.
- **Social Isolation:** The shame and guilt associated with

addiction can lead to social isolation, as the person withdraws from friends, family, and social activities to dedicate themselves to consuming pornography. It's as if they build walls around themselves, isolating in a virtual world that only increases their suffering.

- **Concentration Difficulties:** Constant preoccupation with pornography and the search for new stimuli can impair the ability to concentrate and focus, affecting academic and professional performance. It's as if the mind is always distracted, unable to concentrate on daily tasks.

- **Distorted Body Image:** Exposure to unrealistic and often violent pornographic content can distort a person's perception of sex, relationships, and their own sexuality. It's as if they are looking at the world through a distorted lens, unable to see the beauty and naturalness of real intimacy.

Social and Relational Consequences: Disconnected Roads

Pornography addiction acts as an obstacle in interpersonal relationships, creating difficulties in intimacy, conflicts, and emotional distancing:

- **Intimacy Problems:** Difficulty in emotionally connecting with a real partner and preference for virtual interactions can lead to intimacy issues and hinder the building of healthy relationships. It's as if the person is trying to build bridges with fragile materials that break with each attempt at real closeness.

- **Marital Conflicts:** Pornography addiction can be a source of conflict and tension in marital relationships, generating distrust, jealousy, and resentment. It's as if a dark shadow hovers over the relationship, undermining trust and companionship.

- **Isolation from Family and Friends:** Addiction can lead to isolation from family and friends, harming emotional bonds and social support. It's as if the person is distancing themselves from those who love them, getting lost in a labyrinth of loneliness.

Consequences on Social and Professional Performance: Interrupted Paths

The impact of pornography addiction can extend to the social and professional realms, affecting an individual's performance and responsibilities:

- **Decreased Productivity:** Constant preoccupation with pornography and the time dedicated to its consumption can impair productivity at work or in studies. It's as if the person is carrying an extra burden that prevents them from reaching their maximum potential.
- **Difficulty Maintaining Employment:** In more severe cases, pornography addiction can lead to job loss due to lack of concentration, absenteeism, and inappropriate behavior in the workplace. It's as if the person is sabotaging their own career, unable to control the impulses that lead them down a path of self-destruction.

Final Considerations: A New Beginning

Recognizing the consequences of pornography addiction is the first step toward recovery. It's like lighting a lamp in the labyrinth, revealing the paths that have been walked and the difficulties that have been faced.

Cognitive Behavioral Therapy (CBT) acts as a map and a compass, guiding the person toward the exit of the labyrinth and providing the tools necessary to forge a new path, free from addiction and toward a more fulfilling and satisfying life.

In the following chapters, we will delve deeper into the tools of CBT and other strategies that can assist in overcoming pornography addiction.

CHAPTER 6

Unraveling Cognitive Behavioral Therapy (CBT):
A Guide to Reprogramming Pleasure

Entering the World of CBT

Cognitive Behavioral Therapy (CBT) has proven to be a powerful ally in the journey to recover from pornography addiction. It is like a compass guiding us out of the dark forest of addiction toward a clearer and more satisfying path.

Imagine CBT as a set of tools that allows us to deconstruct the roots of pornography addiction and build a new way of handling pleasure, desire, and sexuality. It is a process of "reprogramming" the brain, where we learn to modify thoughts and behaviors that lead us to compulsive consumption.

In this chapter, we will explore the principles of CBT and how this therapeutic approach can be applied in treating pornography addiction. It is time to unveil the secrets of this compass and tread the path of recovery.

The Pillars of CBT: A Solid Foundation for Change

CBT is based on the idea that our thoughts, emotions, and behaviors are interconnected. It's as if they form a cycle, where each element influences and is influenced by the others. In pornography addiction, this cycle becomes dysfunctional, with distorted thoughts and negative emotions fueling compulsive behavior.

CBT acts on this cycle by identifying and modifying the thoughts and behaviors that sustain the addiction. It's like untangling a blind knot, carefully and patiently unraveling each thread.

Key Principles of CBT:

- **Collaboration:** CBT is a collaborative therapy, where the therapist and the patient work together as a team. It's as if they are building a bridge together, each contributing their part to reach the final goal.
- **Psychoeducation:** The patient learns about pornography addiction, its mechanisms, and its consequences. It's as if they are receiving a map of the forest, with detailed information about the terrain and the dangers that may be encountered.
- **Focus on the Present:** CBT concentrates on the present moment, addressing the difficulties and challenges the patient faces now. It's as if they are learning to navigate the rough terrain ahead, instead of getting stuck in memories of the past.
- **Goal Orientation:** The patient sets clear and specific goals for their recovery. It's as if they are choosing a destination on the map and plotting a course to get there.
- **Skill Learning:** The patient learns skills to handle risky situations, negative emotions, and uncontrollable desires. It's as if they are learning to use the compass tools to navigate the forest.
- **Homework Assignments:** The patient practices the skills learned in therapy in their daily life. It's as if they are exploring the forest on their own, using the map and compass to guide them.

Neuroplasticity: The Ever-Changing Brain

CBT relies on the concept of neuroplasticity, the brain's ability to modify itself in response to new experiences. It's as if the brain is a constantly transforming garden, where new flowers can bloom and old weeds can be removed.

In pornography addiction, the brain adapts to excessive consumption, creating neural pathways that reinforce compulsive behavior. CBT acts by "reprogramming" these pathways, creating new connections that lead to healthier behaviors.

How CBT "Reprograms" the Brain:

- **Identifying Triggers:** The patient learns to recognize the triggers that lead to pornography consumption. It's as if they are identifying the dangerous areas of the forest, where the risk of getting lost is higher.
- **Cognitive Restructuring:** The patient modifies the distorted thoughts that fuel the addiction. It's as if they are clearing the garden of weeds, making space for new flowers to grow.
- **Coping Skills:** The patient develops skills to handle negative emotions and risky situations. It's as if they are learning to use gardening tools to care for the garden and protect it from pests.
- **Relapse Prevention:** The patient creates a plan to avoid relapses and stay on the path of recovery. It's as if they are building a fence around the garden to protect it from wild animals that might destroy the flowers.

Applying CBT to Pornography Addiction: A Step-by-Step Guide

CBT in treating pornography addiction follows a structured

process, which includes:

- **Assessment:** The therapist evaluates the patient, seeking to understand their history, consumption patterns, and challenges. It's as if they are diagnosing the garden, identifying areas that need more attention.
- **Identifying Triggers:** The patient and therapist work together to identify the addiction's triggers. It's as if they are mapping the dangerous areas of the garden, where the risk of getting lost is higher.
- **Monitoring:** The patient monitors their thoughts, emotions, and behaviors. It's as if they are closely observing the garden to identify any signs of problems.
- **Cognitive Restructuring:** The patient learns to challenge and modify their distorted thoughts. It's as if they are learning to remove the weeds from the garden so that the flowers can grow stronger.
- **Coping Skills:** The patient learns skills to handle negative emotions and risky situations. It's as if they are learning to use gardening tools to care for the garden and protect it from pests.
- **Relapse Prevention:** The patient develops a plan to avoid relapses. It's as if they are building a fence around the garden to protect it from wild animals that might destroy the flowers.
- **Positive Sexual Health:** The patient explores a healthier and more pleasurable view of sexuality. It's as if they are learning to cultivate new flowers in the garden that bring beauty and joy.

Final Considerations: A Path of Hope and Transformation

CBT offers a path of hope and transformation for those struggling with pornography addiction. It is like a compass guiding us out of the dark forest of addiction toward a more fulfilling and satisfying life.

Remember, the journey of recovery can be challenging, but with CBT and the support of a professional, it is possible to "reprogram" the brain and forge a new path, free from addiction and toward real and lasting pleasure.

In the following chapters, we will delve deeper into the techniques of CBT and other strategies that can assist in overcoming pornography addiction.

CHAPTER 7

CBT Techniques in Practice: Tools for Reprogramming Pleasure

Building an Arsenal of Skills

In the previous chapter, we explored the principles of Cognitive Behavioral Therapy (CBT) and how this approach can be applied in treating pornography addiction. Now, we will dive into the arsenal of tools and techniques that CBT offers to "reprogram" the brain and tread the path of recovery.

Imagine each CBT technique as a specific tool in a toolbox.

Each tool has a unique and powerful function to help us deconstruct addiction habits and build a new way of handling pleasure, desire, and sexuality.

In this chapter, we will explore each tool in detail, learning how to use them to navigate the challenges of recovery and build a freer and more satisfying life.

1. Identifying Triggers: Mapping the Terrain of Addiction
Unraveling the Triggers of Desire

The first essential tool in our toolbox is trigger identification. Triggers are like "bait" that set off the desire to consume pornography. They can be external, such as a specific environment, an image, or a situation, or internal, such as an emotion, a memory, or a thought.

Imagine you are walking through a forest and come across a familiar trail. This trail has led you to dangerous places before, but you still feel tempted to follow it. Triggers are like that familiar trail: they activate the brain's reward system, awakening desire and compulsion.

Mastering the Art of Identification

CBT teaches us to identify these triggers, like an explorer mapping the terrain to avoid traps and dangers. Through journals, records, and self-observation, we learn to recognize the patterns that lead us to consume pornography.

Exercise:

- **Trigger Diary:** For a week, keep a diary of every time you feel the urge to consume pornography. Also note what was happening before you felt this desire: where you were, who you were with, what you were feeling, and what thoughts were running through your mind.
- **Pattern Analysis:** At the end of the week, review your records and look for patterns. What situations, emotions, or thoughts typically precede the desire to consume pornography?

By identifying your triggers, you are taking the first step to "reprogram" your brain and interrupt the addiction cycle. It's as if you are creating a map of the forest, marking the dangerous trails that should be avoided.

2. Cognitive Restructuring: Rethinking Pleasure

Challenging Distorted Thoughts

The second powerful CBT tool is cognitive restructuring. This technique helps us question and modify the distorted thoughts that fuel pornography addiction.

Imagine you are wearing glasses with distorted lenses. Everything you see looks strange and out of proportion. Distorted thoughts are like these lenses: they make us see pornography as something positive, necessary, or harmless, even when it is causing suffering and destruction.

Rethinking Limiting Beliefs

CBT teaches us to question these distorted thoughts and replace them with more realistic and adaptive thoughts. It's as if we are swapping the distorted lenses for ones that allow us to see reality clearly.

Examples of Distorted Thoughts:

- "I need pornography to relax."
- "I can't control my impulses."
- "Pornography doesn't harm anyone."
- "I am a failure if I can't stop consuming pornography."

Questioning and Reframing:

- "Is pornography the only way to relax? What other activities provide me with pleasure and relaxation?"
- "Can I never control my impulses? In what situations can I exercise self-control?"
- "Does pornography really not harm anyone? What are

the consequences of my pornography consumption for me and those around me?"

- "Am I a failure if I can't stop consuming pornography on my own? What resources and support can I seek to help me?"

Exercise:

- **Identify Your Thoughts:** Write down the distorted thoughts you typically have about pornography.
- **Question Your Thoughts:** Ask yourself questions to challenge the validity of these thoughts.
- **Rewrite Your Thoughts:** Replace distorted thoughts with more realistic and adaptive ones.

By "reprogramming" your thoughts, you are weakening the roots of addiction and paving the way for a new way of handling pleasure and sexuality.

3. Relapse Prevention: Building an Action Plan

Anticipating the Challenges of the Journey

Relapse prevention is a crucial tool in CBT's toolbox. It is like a map guiding us through the challenges of the recovery journey, preparing us to face difficulties and avoid addiction traps.

Imagine you are climbing a mountain. You know the path will be tough and there will be moments of fatigue, doubt, and temptation to give up. Relapse prevention is like an experienced guide accompanying you on this climb, helping you prepare for challenges and stay steadfast on the path.

Developing a Strategic Plan

CBT teaches us to develop a relapse prevention plan by identifying high-risk situations, developing coping strategies, and seeking support when necessary. It's like creating a flight plan, anticipating turbulence, charting alternative routes, and ensuring you have enough fuel to reach the final destination.

Elements of a Relapse Prevention Plan:

- **Identification of High-Risk Situations:** What situations, emotions, or thoughts increase the risk of relapse? It's like identifying the areas with the highest likelihood of turbulence in our flight.
- **Coping Strategies:** What can you do when faced with a high-risk situation? It's like learning to use the airplane's controls to navigate through turbulence.
- **Support Network:** Who can help you during difficult moments? It's like contacting air traffic control for help in an emergency.

Exercise:

- **Create Your Plan:** Develop a relapse prevention plan, including the high-risk situations you identified, the coping strategies you intend to use, and the people you can contact for help.
- **Review Your Plan:** Regularly review your plan and make adjustments when necessary. It's like updating your flight plan according to weather conditions.

By preparing for relapses, you are strengthening your resilience and increasing your chances of success on the recovery journey.

4. Emotional Regulation Techniques: Calming the Inner Storm

Mastering Emotions

Emotions are like waves that come and go, sometimes calm, sometimes turbulent. In pornography addiction, negative emotions such as anxiety, sadness, and anger can be powerful triggers for compulsive consumption. It's as if these emotions are storms that divert us from our course and lead us back to the dangerous addiction trails.

CBT equips us with emotional regulation techniques to "calm the inner storm" and navigate emotions with greater serenity. It's like learning to surf the waves, maintaining balance and direction even amidst turbulence.

Emotional Regulation Techniques:

- **Mindfulness:** The practice of mindfulness teaches us to observe emotions without judgment, with acceptance and compassion. It's like watching the sea waves without being swept away by the current.
- **Relaxation:** Relaxation techniques, such as deep breathing and progressive muscle relaxation, help reduce physical and emotional tension. It's like anchoring the boat in a safe harbor, waiting for the storm to pass.
- **Assertive Communication:** Learning to express your emotions clearly and respectfully helps avoid conflicts and build healthier relationships. It's like learning to use hand signals to communicate with other boats, avoiding collisions and navigating harmoniously.

Exercise:
- **Practice Mindfulness:** Set aside a few minutes each day to practice mindfulness, observing your breath, your thoughts, and your emotions without judgment.
- **Try Relaxation Techniques:** Experiment with different relaxation techniques, such as deep breathing, guided

> meditation, and progressive muscle relaxation, and find the ones that work best for you.
> - **Communicate Assertively:** Practice assertive communication in your daily interactions, expressing your needs and emotions clearly and respectfully.

By mastering emotional regulation tools, you are strengthening your ability to handle the waves of addiction and navigating toward a calmer and more balanced life.

5. Exposure and Response Prevention (ERP): Facing Fear

Unraveling ERP

Exposure and Response Prevention (ERP) is an advanced CBT technique that helps us confront the fear and anxiety associated with pornography addiction. It's like entering a dark room with a flashlight, illuminating the shadowy corners and dispelling the imaginary monsters that haunt us.

Imagine you are afraid of heights. ERP would gradually take you to increasingly higher places while teaching you to cope with the anxiety and fear. In pornography addiction, ERP involves gradual exposure to pornography-related stimuli without engaging in compulsive behavior.

Weakening the Chains of Addiction

This controlled and gradual exposure helps desensitize the brain to stimuli that trigger desire, weakening the chains of addiction. It's like slowly approaching the cliff, learning to cope with the feeling of vertigo until it loses the power to paralyze you.

Applying ERP with Caution

ERP is a powerful technique but should be applied cautiously and with professional guidance. It's like exploring unknown territory with the help of an experienced guide who ensures your safety and support.

Final Considerations: Building a Life Free from Addiction

CBT techniques are powerful tools for "reprogramming" the brain and overcoming pornography addiction. It's like learning to use a set of tools to build a new life, free from addiction and full of possibilities.

Remember, the recovery journey can be challenging, but with the right tools and professional support, you can forge a new path toward a more fulfilling, healthy, and satisfying life.

In the following chapters, we will delve deeper into CBT techniques and other strategies that can assist in overcoming pornography addiction.

CHAPTER 8

Adapting CBT: A Look into Individual Needs

The Beauty of Diversity and the Adaptability of CBT

Just as each person is unique, with their own stories, challenges, and characteristics, pornography addiction also manifests differently in each individual. Cognitive Behavioral Therapy (CBT), recognizing this individuality, offers the flexibility to adapt its tools and techniques to meet each person's specific needs.

Imagine CBT as a set of clothes that can be adjusted to fit perfectly on different bodies. It is necessary to consider each person's measurements, style, and preferences so that the clothing fits in the best possible way.

In this chapter, we will explore how CBT can be adapted for different populations, including adolescents, couples, and individuals with coexisting mental disorders (comorbidities).

1. Adolescents: Developing Brain, Unique Challenges
The Challenge of Adolescence

Adolescence is a phase of significant transformations, with the brain still developing and the search for identity and new experiences. Pornography addiction can be particularly challenging during this phase, as the adolescent brain is more sensitive to the rewarding effects of pornography and does not yet possess the same level of inhibitory control as an adult.

It's as if adolescents are learning to drive on a road full of curves and obstacles, with a powerful car and brakes still under development.

Adapting CBT for Adolescents

CBT for adolescents must consider the specific characteristics of this phase, such as impulsivity, the search for social approval, and peer influence. Therapy sessions can be shorter and more dynamic, with activities and games that engage the adolescent and help them understand CBT concepts in a more playful manner.

It's as if we are teaching them to drive with a simulator, allowing the adolescent to practice their skills in a safe and controlled environment.

Family Involvement: An Essential Pillar

Family involvement is crucial in treating adolescents with pornography addiction. CBT can help the family understand the problem, develop support strategies, and build a healthier and more protective family environment.

It's as if we are providing a map and compass to the family, guiding them on the adolescent's recovery journey.

2. Couples: Healing Wounds, Rebuilding Bridges

The Impact of Addiction on the Relationship

Pornography addiction can cause great suffering in romantic relationships, generating distrust, hurt, and emotional distancing. CBT for couples seeks to rebuild intimacy and trust, helping the couple communicate more openly and honestly, handle emotions, and build a new foundation for the relationship.

It's as if we are rebuilding a bridge that was damaged by the storm, creating a stronger and more resilient structure for the future.

Adapting CBT for Couples

CBT for couples involves both joint and individual sessions, addressing each partner's specific needs. The focus is on rebuilding trust, improving communication, and developing strategies to manage addiction together.

It's as if we are teaching the couple to dance a new dance, with more harmonious and synchronized steps.

Forgive, Heal, and Rebuild

CBT can also help the couple deal with the emotional wounds caused by addiction, promoting forgiveness, healing, and the rebuilding of intimacy.

It's as if we are tending to the wounds with remedies and bandages, allowing the couple to embrace with more comfort and security.

3. Individuals with Comorbidities: An Integrated Approach

Complex Challenges, Comprehensive Approach

Many individuals struggling with pornography addiction also face other mental disorders, such as depression, anxiety, and Obsessive-Compulsive Disorder (OCD). CBT for individuals with comorbidities requires an integrated approach that considers the specific needs of each disorder.

It's as if we are treating a garden with different types of plants, each requiring specific care to thrive.

Adapting CBT for Individuals with Comorbidities

CBT for individuals with comorbidities may involve combining techniques to address both pornography addiction and other disorders. The goal is to promote complete and lasting recovery that addresses all aspects of the individual's mental health.

It's as if we are tending to the soil, water, and light of the garden so that all plants can grow and prosper.

Final Considerations: The Importance of Individualization

CBT is a flexible and adaptable therapeutic approach that can be tailored to meet each person's individual needs. It's like a chameleon changing color to camouflage in different environments.

By recognizing each person's individuality, CBT increases its chances of success, guiding the individual on the journey to recover from pornography addiction and build a freer and more satisfying life.

CHAPTER 9

The Strength of Evidence: CBT and the Treatment of Pornography Addiction - A Critical Analysis

Cognitive Behavioral Therapy (CBT) stands out as a promising approach in the treatment of pornography addiction, with increasing scientific evidence supporting its efficacy. This chapter delves into current research, critically analyzing studies that demonstrate the effectiveness of CBT, exploring its mechanisms of action, and outlining future directions for research.

Unraveling the Results: An Overview of Studies

The effectiveness of CBT in treating pornography addiction is corroborated by various studies, although methodological quality varies (Brand et al., 2016). These studies demonstrate CBT's ability to:

- **Reduce Pornography Consumption:** Studies show a significant decrease in the frequency and duration of pornography consumption in individuals undergoing CBT compared to control groups (Laier et al., 2014). This reduction is often accompanied by improvements in quality of life and relationships.

- **Minimize Compulsive Behaviors:** CBT assists in reducing compulsive behaviors associated with addiction, such as excessive masturbation and the constant search for new pornographic stimuli (Grant et al., 2010). The intervention focuses on developing self-control and coping strategies.

- **Alleviate Cravings:** CBT demonstrates effectiveness in reducing the intensity and frequency of cravings for pornography, equipping individuals with strategies to manage these impulses (Cyders & Smith, 2008). Techniques like mindfulness and cognitive restructuring are fundamental in this process.

- **Improve Psychological Well-Being:** Beyond reducing problematic behaviors, CBT promotes significant improvements in psychological well-being, decreasing symptoms of anxiety, depression, and increasing self-esteem (Brand et al., 2016). Enhanced overall well-being contributes to the maintenance of therapeutic gains.

Meta-Analyses: An Expanded Perspective

Meta-analyses, which combine results from multiple studies, offer an expanded perspective on the efficacy of CBT (e.g., Brand et al., 2016). Although the number of meta-analyses specific to pornography addiction is limited, meta-analyses on behavioral addictions in general demonstrate the effectiveness of cognitive-behavioral approaches. They help identify the most effective components of CBT and guide future research directions. However, the heterogeneity of studies limits the strength of the conclusions.

Inside the Brain: The Mechanisms of CBT Action

Research seeks to understand how CBT produces its effects. Although neuroimaging studies specific to CBT in pornography addiction are limited, research on CBT in other behavioral addictions suggests changes in crucial brain areas (e.g., Koob & Volkow, 2010):

- **Prefrontal Cortex:** CBT strengthens the activity of the prefrontal cortex, the region responsible for executive control, decision-making, and impulse inhibition, allowing greater control over behavior.
- **Amygdala:** CBT may modulate the hyperactivity of the amygdala, reducing reactivity to pornographic stimuli and the intensity of emotional responses associated with addiction.
- **Reward Circuitry:** CBT modulates the brain's reward circuitry, decreasing sensitivity to pornographic stimuli and reducing the compulsive pursuit of immediate gratification.

Gaps and Horizons: The Future of Research

Despite the evidence, research on CBT in the treatment of pornography addiction presents gaps:

- **More Representative Samples:** Studies with larger and more diverse samples are needed to ensure the generalizability of results.
- **Comorbidities and Maintenance Factors:** More research is required to investigate the efficacy of CBT in individuals with comorbidities and to identify factors that contribute to the maintenance of addiction in the long term.
- **Enhancement of Protocols:** More specific and standardized CBT protocols will allow greater replicability of studies and comparison between different interventions.
- **Emerging Technologies:** Incorporating emerging technologies, such as virtual reality and artificial intelligence, may expand the reach and effectiveness of CBT.

Final Considerations: Strengthening the Evidence Base

CBT has emerged as a versatile and effective approach in the treatment of pornography addiction, supported by a growing body of scientific evidence. However, to solidify its standing, further research addressing current gaps is essential. Enhancing methodological quality, expanding sample diversity, and integrating new technologies will contribute to a more comprehensive understanding of CBT's efficacy and mechanisms.

By continuing to build a robust evidence base, CBT can be refined and optimized to better serve individuals struggling with pornography addiction, ultimately paving the way for more effective and personalized treatment strategies.

CHAPTER 10

**Integrating Approaches:
A Holistic View of Pornography Addiction Treatment**

The Pursuit of a Comprehensive and Personalized Treatment

Cognitive Behavioral Therapy (CBT) stands out as a cornerstone in the treatment of pornography addiction, offering effective tools to modify dysfunctional thoughts and behaviors. However, the complexity of addiction and the individuality of each person require exploring the integration of CBT with other therapeutic approaches.

Imagine a puzzle where CBT is a fundamental piece, but other pieces are also necessary to complete the picture. Integrating different therapeutic approaches allows for constructing a more comprehensive and personalized treatment that meets each individual's specific needs.

In this chapter, we will explore how combining CBT with other therapies can enhance recovery and promote more comprehensive well-being.

1. CBT and Couples Therapy: Healing Wounds, Rebuilding Bridges

The Impact of Addiction on the Relationship

Pornography addiction can cause significant suffering in romantic relationships, generating distrust, hurt, and emotional distancing. Combining individual CBT with couples therapy is crucial for rebuilding intimacy, trust, and communication.

It's as if the couple is learning to dance a new dance, with more harmonious and synchronized steps.

Combining CBT with Couples Therapy

Couples therapy, in this context, seeks to:

- **Create a Safe Space for Dialogue:** Facilitate open and honest communication between partners, allowing them to express emotions, fears, and expectations without judgment.
- **Restore Lost Trust:** Address the breach of trust caused by addiction, working on forgiveness, accountability, and commitment to change.
- **Demystify Sexuality:** Educate the couple about healthy sexuality, dismantling dysfunctional myths and beliefs that may be fueling the addiction.
- **Rebuild Intimacy:** Foster emotional and physical intimacy, encouraging affectionate contact, non-verbal communication, and the exploration of new forms of shared pleasure.
- **Negotiate Boundaries and Agreements:** Assist the couple in establishing healthy boundaries regarding technology use and online content consumption.

2. CBT and Pharmacotherapy: A Biopsychosocial Approach

In some cases, combining CBT with pharmacotherapy can be beneficial in treating pornography addiction. Pharmacotherapy, prescribed and monitored by a psychiatrist, can assist in managing:

- **Psychiatric Comorbidities:** Disorders such as depression, anxiety, and Obsessive-Compulsive Disorder (OCD) often coexist with pornography addiction. Pharmacotherapy can alleviate symptoms of these comorbidities, facilitating engagement in CBT.
- **Neurochemical Dysregulation:** Pornography addiction can lead to neurochemical imbalances in the brain. Specific medications can help restore balance, reducing cravings and compulsions.

3. CBT and Mindfulness: Cultivating Presence and Awareness

The practice of mindfulness, with its emphasis on present-moment awareness and non-judgmental acceptance, complements CBT in treating pornography addiction.

It's as if the person is learning to observe the sea waves without being swept away by the current.

Integrating Mindfulness Allows:
- **Observing Thoughts and Emotions Without Reacting:** Developing the ability to observe thoughts and emotions related to addiction without being carried away by them, reducing reactivity and impulsivity.
- **Precisely Identifying Triggers:** Increasing awareness of internal and external triggers that spark the desire for pornography.
- **Tolerating the Discomfort of Cravings:** Building the skill to handle the anxiety and discomfort associated with cravings without resorting to compulsive behavior.
- **Connecting with the Present:** Bringing focus to the present moment, reducing rumination about the past and worries about the future that can fuel addiction.

4. CBT and Acceptance and Commitment Therapy (ACT):

Aligning Values and Actions

Acceptance and Commitment Therapy (ACT) shares with CBT the emphasis on behavioral change but adds a focus on personal values. Integrating ACT with CBT helps individuals to:

- **Clarify Their Values:** Identify what is truly important in their lives, such as healthy relationships, personal growth, and spirituality.
- **Align Their Actions with Their Values:** Act in accordance with their values, even in the face of difficulties and temptations.
- **Accept Internal Experiences:** Develop the ability to accept unpleasant thoughts, emotions, and sensations without becoming entangled with them, allowing focus on acting in line with their values.

Final Considerations: The Importance of Individualization

Combining CBT with other therapeutic approaches offers a more comprehensive and personalized path to recovering from pornography addiction.

It's like building a house with different materials and tools, each with its function and importance.

The key to effective treatment is individualization, considering the person's life history, personality traits, severity of addiction, presence of comorbidities, and patient preferences.

It's as if we are creating a unique and special garden, with flowers and plants that adapt to the local climate, soil, and light.

Remember, the recovery journey can be challenging, but with the right tools and professional support, it is possible to forge a new path toward a more fulfilling, healthy, and satisfying life.

CHAPTER 11

Diving into Psychoanalysis: An Inner Journey in Search of Freedom

Beyond Thoughts and Behaviors: Exploring the Unconscious

Throughout this book, we have navigated pornography addiction using the compass of Cognitive Behavioral Therapy (CBT), focusing on how our thoughts and behaviors shape this experience. But what if we sail into different waters, exploring the deep sea of the unconscious?

Psychoanalysis, with its emphasis on hidden desires, internal conflicts, and past experiences, offers a perspective that complements CBT. It is as if psychoanalysis were a deep dive into the ocean of the mind, seeking the submerged roots of pornography addiction.

In this chapter, we will immerse ourselves in psychoanalysis and its application in treating pornography addiction, unraveling its mysteries and potential.

Unveiling the Unconscious Iceberg

Psychoanalysis, founded by Sigmund Freud in the late 19th century, operates on the premise that a large part of our mental life is influenced by unconscious forces, repressed desires, and internal conflicts. It's as if our mind were an iceberg, with most of its mass submerged, invisible to the naked eye, yet exerting a strong influence over the visible part.

In the context of pornography addiction, psychoanalysis seeks to understand the unconscious motivations that fuel compulsive consumption. It's as if the addiction were a symptom, a visible manifestation of a deeper malaise hidden in the depths of the unconscious.

Pornography Addiction from a Psychoanalytic Perspective

Psychoanalysis offers different lenses to understand pornography addiction:

- **Unconscious Conflicts:** The addiction may be a way of dealing with unconscious conflicts related to sexuality, shame, guilt, or past traumas. It's as if the person is fighting an internal battle, and pornography serves as a way to avoid direct confrontation with their deepest fears and desires.
- **Fixation in Developmental Stages:** Some psychoanalytic authors suggest that addiction may be related to a fixation in stages of psychosexual development, such as the oral, anal, or phallic stages. It's as if the person is stuck in a particular moment of their history, seeking satisfaction in pornography that they did not find in past experiences.
- **Compulsive Repetition:** The addiction can be understood as a way of compulsively repeating patterns of relationships or traumatic past experiences. It's as if the person is trapped in a vicious cycle, unconsciously reliving painful situations in an attempt to find resolution.

Psychoanalytic Treatment: A Journey of Self-Discovery

Psychoanalytic treatment of pornography addiction resembles an archaeological expedition in search of hidden treasures and answers in the depths of the mind. The goal is to bring to light the unconscious conflicts and past experiences that contribute to the compulsive behavior.

Through dream analysis, free associations, and the therapeutic relationship (transference), the patient, guided by the psychoanalyst, can unravel the mysteries of their unconscious, work through their conflicts, and free themselves from the behavioral patterns that imprison them in addiction.

Final Considerations: The Power of Integration

Psychoanalysis and CBT, as different vessels, can navigate together in the ocean of the mind, each with its own routes and tools, in search of overcoming pornography addiction.

While CBT acts as a detailed map, guiding the patient through clear and defined routes, psychoanalysis functions like a compass, orienting the exploration of the mind's depths and the discovery of submerged treasures.

Integrating psychoanalysis with CBT and other therapeutic approaches offers a more comprehensive and personalized treatment, considering the uniqueness of each individual and their specific needs.

It is essential for the person seeking treatment to find a qualified and experienced professional who can guide them in choosing the best therapeutic approach for their recovery journey.

CHAPTER 12

Preventing Pornography Addiction: A Collective Effort for a Healthy Future

Building a Future Free from Addiction: A Collective Challenge

Pornography addiction, like a weed spreading through a garden, represents a growing challenge in the digital age, with profound implications for individuals, relationships, and public health. To combat this problem, we need to go beyond treatment, focusing on prevention and building a healthier and more conscious future.

Imagine prevention as building a wall around the garden, protecting it from the seeds of addiction. It is a collective effort that requires participation from various sectors of society: governments, schools, families, and communities.

In this chapter, we will explore prevention strategies for pornography addiction, building a future where sexuality is experienced in a fuller, healthier, and more responsible manner.

Comprehensive Sexual Education: Planting Seeds of Awareness

Comprehensive and quality sexual education, initiated in childhood and continued throughout life, is the foundation for preventing pornography addiction. It is like preparing the garden soil, cultivating a fertile environment for the development of healthy attitudes and behaviors.

This education should go beyond mere information about biology and reproduction, encompassing:

- **Understanding Human Sexuality:** Promoting a holistic view of sexuality that includes biological, psychological, social, and cultural aspects. It's like watering the garden wisely, nurturing the growth of a balanced and integrated sexuality.
- **Developing Healthy Relationships:** Teaching skills to build and maintain healthy interpersonal relationships based on respect, communication, empathy, and consent. It's like pruning the garden plants, removing branches that hinder growth and connection.
- **Media Literacy and Critical Thinking:** Developing the ability to critically analyze messages conveyed by the media, including pornography. It's like protecting the garden from pests, teaching plants to defend themselves against harmful influences.
- **Risks and Consequences of Excessive Consumption:** Clearly and objectively informing about the risks of pornography addiction, such as sexual dysfunction, distorted body image, social isolation, and mental health issues. It's like placing warning signs in the garden, alerting to dangers and areas of care.
- **Help and Support Resources:** Disseminating information on where to seek help in case of difficulties related to pornography consumption. It's like having a first aid kit in the garden, to care for wounds and ensure the health of the plants.

Developing Socioemotional Skills: Strengthening the Roots

Individuals with well-developed socioemotional skills are more resilient and less vulnerable to risky behaviors, including pornography addiction. It's like strengthening the roots of plants, making them more resistant to storms and environmental challenges.

Prevention should focus on developing:

- **Self-Esteem and Self-Confidence:** Believing in oneself, recognizing one's value and capabilities. It's like nourishing plants with fertilizer, strengthening their growth and development.
- **Assertiveness:** Expressing opinions and needs clearly and respectfully. It's like giving space for plants to grow, allowing them to expand and occupy their place in the garden.
- **Emotional Regulation:** Handling emotions in a healthy and balanced way. It's like controlling the amount of water and light plants receive, ensuring they have the ideal environment to flourish.
- **Problem-Solving:** Finding creative solutions to life's challenges. It's like removing stones from the path, allowing plant roots to deepen and find nutrients.
- **Responsible Decision-Making:** Making conscious choices aligned with one's values. It's like choosing the right plants for the garden, considering their needs and characteristics.

Creating Safe and Healthy Environments: Caring for the Garden

Preventing pornography addiction also requires creating healthy and protective environments, both online and offline. It's like taking care of the garden's soil, water, and light, ensuring that plants have everything they need to grow and thrive.

Some important actions to create safer environments include:

- **Restricting Minors' Access:** Implementing measures

to limit children's and adolescents' access to online pornographic content. It's like building a fence around the garden, protecting it from intruders.

- **Holding Digital Platforms Accountable:** Encouraging online platforms to adopt stricter content moderation practices and to provide support resources to users. It's like hiring an experienced gardener to tend the garden, removing weeds and ensuring the health of the plants.
- **Open Dialogue in Families:** Creating a family environment where sexuality can be discussed openly and honestly. It's like talking to the plants, understanding their needs and providing appropriate care.
- **Community Engagement:** Mobilizing communities in preventing pornography addiction by promoting educational and informative activities. It's like creating a community garden, where everyone takes responsibility for the care and beauty of the space.

Final Considerations: Cultivating a Healthier Future

Preventing pornography addiction is a collective commitment that requires collaboration from different sectors of society.

It's like tending to a garden, a task that demands dedication, patience, and love.

By investing in comprehensive sexual education, developing socioemotional skills, and creating safer and healthier environments, we are planting the seeds for a more promising future, where sexuality is experienced in a fuller, more conscious, and responsible way.

CHAPTER 13

Ethical and Social Considerations: Navigating Turbulent Waters

Pornography addiction, beyond its individual implications, invites us to a profound reflection on its impacts on society and to navigate the turbulent waters of the ethical issues that surround it. It is as if the addiction were a lighthouse, illuminating dilemmas and challenges that require attention and responsibility.

In this chapter, we will explore the ethical and social implications of pornography addiction, critically analyzing individual and collective responsibilities, and seeking solutions for a more ethical and just future.

The Pornographic Industry: A Sea of Exploitation?

The pornographic industry, with its influential power and global reach, plays a central role in this discussion. It is as if it were a giant ship navigating turbulent waters, with the potential to generate waves that impact the lives of millions of people.

It is crucial to question the practices and values that sustain this industry, critically analyzing issues such as:

- **Exploitation and Abuse:** The production of pornography, in many cases, involves the exploitation and abuse of actors and actresses, who may be subjected to degrading working conditions, violence, and coercion. It is as if the ship were carrying a heavy burden of suffering and injustice.

- **Objectification and Dehumanization:** Pornography often portrays people as sexual objects, dehumanizing them and perpetuating harmful gender stereotypes. It is as if the ship were transporting a dangerous cargo that contaminates the waters it traverses.

- **Hypersexualization of Culture:** The ubiquity of pornography on the internet contributes to the hypersexualization of culture, influencing how people relate to sexuality and their own bodies. It is as if the ship were emitting waves that distort the surrounding landscape.

Individual Responsibility: Choosing Our Routes

Amidst this turbulent sea, each individual has the responsibility to choose their routes and navigate with awareness and ethics. It is as if each person were a small boat, with the power to decide where they want to go and how they want to get there.

Some important reflections on individual responsibility include:

- **Conscious Consumption:** Questioning the content we consume, prioritizing ethical productions that respect human rights. It is like choosing to sail in calmer waters, avoiding polluted and dangerous areas.

- **Mental Health Care:** Seeking help in case of difficulties with pornography addiction, prioritizing physical and mental well-being. It is like equipping the boat with the necessary navigation instruments to face storms.

- **Open Dialogue:** Talking about pornography addiction with friends, family, and partners, promoting awareness and mutual support. It is like communicating with other boats, sharing information and sailing together.

Collective Responsibility: Changing the Course of History

Preventing and combating pornography addiction requires a collective effort, with participation from different sectors of society. It is as if all the boats joined together to change the course of history, building a more just and sustainable future.

Some important actions for collective responsibility include:

- **Education and Awareness:** Promoting comprehensive sexual education and raising awareness about the risks of pornography addiction. It is like building lighthouses that guide boats, alerting to dangers and illuminating the path.
- **Regulation of the Industry:** Creating laws and regulations that protect the rights of actors and actresses in the pornographic industry and combat exploitation and abuse. It is like establishing navigation rules, ensuring safety and respect for all.
- **Development of Public Policies:** Implementing public policies that promote mental health and the well-being of the population, focusing on preventing pornography addiction. It is like creating a navigation map that takes into account the needs of all boats.

Final Considerations: Towards a More Ethical Horizon

Pornography addiction challenges us to rethink our values and build a more ethical and responsible future. It is as if we were sailing in a sea of transformations, in search of a fairer and more sustainable horizon.

By questioning the practices of the pornographic industry, assuming our individual responsibilities, and working together for social change, we are building a future where sexuality is experienced with more freedom, awareness, and respect.

CHAPTER 14

Behind the Camera: Unveiling the Truth About the Pornographic Industry

A Look Beyond Fantasy:

In the previous chapter, we began an important reflection on the ethical and social implications of pornography addiction. Now, we will deepen this analysis by turning our gaze to the pornographic industry and unveiling the truth that lies behind the cameras.

It is as if we were pulling back the curtains of a stage, revealing the backstage and the gears that drive this multibillion-dollar industry, which exerts significant influence over culture, sexuality, and relationships.

Myths and Realities:

The pornographic industry, with its bright lights and seductive fantasies, often perpetuates a series of myths about sex, pleasure, and relationships. It is as if it creates a world of illusions, distorting reality and perpetuating unrealistic expectations.

Let's debunk some of these myths:

- **Myth 1: Pornography is Harmless:**

The pornographic industry often presents itself as a harmless form of entertainment, but the reality is quite different. Studies show that exposure to pornography can have negative impacts on mental health, relationships, and individuals' sexuality. It is as if the industry is selling a product with a false label, hiding its side effects.

- **Myth 2: Actors and Actresses are Happy and Fulfilled:**

The pornographic industry often portrays its actors and actresses as happy, fulfilled individuals who freely choose to participate in productions. However, the reality is that many of them face exploitation, abuse, mental health issues, and financial difficulties. It is as if the industry is hiding the faces behind the masks, ignoring the suffering and vulnerability of its workers.

- **Myth 3: Pornography Reflects Real Sexuality:**

Pornography creates a distorted and unrealistic representation of sexuality, focusing on extreme performances, violence, and objectification. This distortion can generate unrealistic expectations about sex and relationships, leading to dissatisfaction, anxiety, and sexual dysfunctions. It is as if the industry is selling a fake map that leads people to get lost in unknown and dangerous territory.

The Dark Side of the Industry:

The pornographic industry, in many cases, operates on the margins of ethics and legality, with practices that violate human rights and perpetuate exploitation and abuse. It is as if it were navigating dark waters, away from the eyes of justice and compassion.

Some of the industry's most serious problems include:

- **Human Trafficking:**

The pornographic industry is one of the main destinations for victims of human trafficking, who are forced to perform sexual acts on camera. It is as if the ship were transporting modern slaves, trapped in a cycle of exploitation and violence.

- **Sexual Abuse:**

Many actors and actresses in the pornographic industry report having suffered sexual abuse during filming. It is as if the stage transforms into a battlefield, where violence and humiliation are normalized.

- **Financial Exploitation:**
Actors and actresses in the pornographic industry often receive low wages and have no guaranteed labor rights. It is as if the industry is profiting from the sweat and suffering of its workers without offering fair and dignified conditions.

- **Mental Health Issues:**

Studies show that actors and actresses in the pornographic industry have a higher prevalence of mental health problems, such as depression, anxiety, eating disorders, and substance abuse. It is as if the industry is leaving a trail of destruction in the lives of its workers, marking them with deep and invisible scars.

Responsibility and Change:

Given this reality, it is crucial to question our roles as consumers and citizens. It is as if we were faced with a map, with the power to choose new routes and build a more just and ethical future.

Some actions we can take include:

- **Consume Pornography Consciously:**

Prioritize ethical productions that respect human rights and promote gender equality. It is like choosing to sail in cleaner waters, supporting companies that care about their workers' well-being and the social impact of their products.

- **Support Organizations Fighting Exploitation:**
Contribute to organizations that combat human trafficking and sexual abuse in the pornographic industry. It is like throwing life buoys to those who are drowning, offering help and hope.

- **Promote Comprehensive Sexual Education:**

Encourage comprehensive and quality sexual education that promotes gender equality, mutual respect, and the development of healthy relationships. It is like building a new ship equipped with more precise and safe navigation instruments, leading us to a more promising future.

- **Demand Industry Accountability:**

Hold technology companies and online platforms accountable by urging them to adopt stricter measures to combat exploitation and abuse in the pornographic industry. It is like demanding that the ship follows maritime laws, ensuring everyone's safety on board.

Final Considerations:

The pornographic industry, with its lights and shadows, invites us to a profound reflection on sexuality, power, and ethics. It is as if we were sailing in a sea of challenges, in search of a fairer and more humane horizon.

By unveiling the truth behind the cameras, questioning the myths, and assuming our responsibilities, we are building a future where pleasure and sexuality are experienced with more respect, awareness, and freedom.

CHAPTER 15

Decades of Exposure to Pornography: What Do Studies Say and Future Perspectives?

The Constantly Transforming Brain:

The human brain is an extraordinary organ, capable of adapting and reshaping itself throughout life, a phenomenon known as neuroplasticity. This capacity for change, while essential for learning and development, also makes the brain vulnerable to the effects of prolonged exposure to intense stimuli, such as those provided by pornography.

Imagine the brain as a constantly transforming forest, with trails and paths that change with each new experience. Exposure to pornography, especially over decades, can mold this forest in a deep and lasting way, creating neural pathways that reinforce addiction and hinder recovery.

What Do Studies Say?

Although research on the effects of prolonged exposure to pornography is still relatively recent, some studies point to significant consequences for the brain:

- **Changes in the Reward System:** Chronic exposure to

pornography can lead to desensitization of the reward system, making the brain less sensitive to natural sources of pleasure. It's as if the forest becomes accustomed to a specific type of rain, becoming less receptive to other forms of irrigation.

- **Increased Sensitization:** Repeated exposure to pornographic stimuli can increase the brain's sensitization to these stimuli, making the individual more vulnerable to cravings and relapses. It's as if the forest becomes more sensitive to a specific type of seed, facilitating the growth of weeds.

- **Reduction in Gray Matter:** Some studies indicate that prolonged exposure to pornography may be associated with a reduction in gray matter in areas of the brain related to inhibitory control and decision-making. It's as if some trees in the forest are losing their leaves, weakening their structure and ability to withstand the winds.

- **Impact on Relationships:** Exposure to pornography can affect the ability to form and maintain healthy intimate relationships, as it distorts expectations and perceptions of sexuality. It's as if the forest is becoming isolated, making it difficult to connect with other forests.

Future Perspectives:

Research on the effects of prolonged exposure to pornography is still ongoing, with new discoveries being made every day. It's as if we are exploring unknown territory, unraveling its mysteries, and seeking solutions to the challenges we encounter.

Some of the questions researchers are seeking to answer include:

- **What are the effects of pornography exposure during adolescence, a phase of significant brain development?**
- **How does prolonged exposure to pornography affect sexual function and long-term relationships?**

- **Is it possible to reverse the effects of prolonged pornography exposure on the brain?**
- **What are the best prevention and treatment strategies for pornography addiction, considering different levels of exposure?**

A Call to Action:

Understanding the effects of prolonged exposure to pornography on the brain is crucial for the prevention and treatment of addiction. It's as if we are learning to care for the forest, protecting it from dangers and ensuring its health and vitality.

Investment in research, promotion of comprehensive sexual education, and the development of public policies aimed at building a healthier and more conscious future are essential. This future envisions sexuality being experienced with greater freedom, responsibility, and respect.

CHAPTER 16

Spirituality and Recovery from Pornography Addiction: A Scientific Perspective

Beyond the Mind and Body: The Search for Meaning and Connection:

Throughout this book, we have explored pornography addiction from various perspectives, ranging from neuroscience to psychoanalysis, from Cognitive Behavioral Therapy (CBT) to the importance of relationships. But what if the recovery journey also involved a spiritual dimension?

Spirituality, often defined as the search for meaning, purpose, and connection with something greater than oneself, has been identified as an important factor in the recovery from various mental and behavioral disorders, including pornography addiction.

Imagine spirituality as a compass guiding the recovery journey, helping the individual find direction, strength, and hope amid the challenges of addiction.

In this chapter, we will explore the importance of spirituality in recovering from pornography addiction, based on scientific evidence and recent findings.

Spirituality and Mental Well-Being:

Scientific studies have demonstrated a strong correlation between spirituality and mental well-being. Individuals who consider themselves spiritual tend to exhibit lower levels of depression, anxiety, and stress, as well as greater resilience and the ability to cope with adversity.

Spirituality can provide a sense of purpose and meaning in life, helping individuals connect with something greater than themselves and find hope in times of difficulty.

Spirituality and Addiction:

In the context of addiction, spirituality can act as a protective factor, reducing the likelihood of developing addiction and increasing the chances of recovery.

Individuals who rely on their faith or spiritual beliefs during addiction treatment tend to achieve better outcomes, with a higher likelihood of abstinence and a lower risk of relapse.

How Spirituality Helps in Recovering from Pornography Addiction:

Spirituality can assist in recovering from pornography addiction in various ways:

- **Finding Meaning and Purpose:**

Spirituality can help individuals find a sense of purpose and meaning in life that goes beyond the pursuit of immediate pleasure and instant gratification.

- **Developing Self-Knowledge:**

Spirituality can promote self-awareness and introspection, helping individuals understand their motivations, values, and beliefs.

- **Strengthening Human Connection:**

Spirituality can strengthen human connections and the sense of community, providing social and emotional support.

- **Cultivating Compassion and Forgiveness:**

Spirituality can help individuals cultivate compassion for themselves and others, forgiving themselves for their mistakes and finding inner peace.

- **Connecting with Nature:**

Spirituality can manifest in the connection with nature, finding beauty and peace in the natural world.

Integrating Spirituality into Treatment:

Spirituality can be integrated into the treatment of pornography addiction in various ways:

- **Meditative and Contemplative Practices:**

Meditation, prayer, and other contemplative practices can help individuals connect with themselves and something greater than themselves.

- **Participation in Religious or Spiritual Groups:**

Participating in religious or spiritual groups can offer social support, guidance, and a sense of community.

- **Reading Sacred or Inspirational Texts:**

Reading sacred or inspirational texts can provide comfort, hope, and guidance.

- **Connection with Nature:**

Connecting with nature through activities like hiking, gardening, or other outdoor activities can promote inner peace and well-being.

Final Considerations:

Spirituality, with its ability to promote mental well-being, self-knowledge, and human connection, can be a powerful ally in recovering from pornography addiction.

It is important to respect each individual's uniqueness and their relationship with spirituality, offering different paths and practices that can assist in the recovery journey.

Remember, spirituality can be a compass guiding the recovery journey, but the map and the steps of the journey are unique to each person.

CHAPTER 17

A Message of Hope: You Are Not Alone!

If you are reading this message, it is likely that you are facing a difficult battle against pornography addiction. Your thoughts may be clouded by guilt and shame, and the feeling of being trapped in a vicious cycle might seem overwhelming. But we want you to know: you are not alone!

The journey of recovery can be challenging, with obstacles and setbacks along the way. But we want to remind you that recovery is possible. Just as many have walked this path and found freedom, you can too.

Believe in Your Ability to Change:

Your brain, with its incredible capacity to adapt and reprogram itself, is your greatest ally on this journey. With each step you take toward recovery, new trails and neural connections will form, guiding you toward a healthier and more fulfilling life.

Seek Support and Knowledge:

Don't hesitate to seek professional help. Psychotherapy, with its effective tools and strategies, can be your compass on this journey, guiding you through challenges and helping you "reprogram" your brain.

Remember That You Are Stronger Than You Think:

You possess an inner strength that can propel you beyond obstacles. Cultivate self-compassion, acknowledge your progress, and celebrate each achievement, no matter how small.

Find Support in Others:

Share your journey with friends, family, or support groups. Knowing that you are not alone can make all the difference.

Embrace Spirituality:

If spirituality is part of your life, seek strength, hope, and connection in it.

Build a Life with Purpose:

Rediscover your values, dreams, and passions. Build a life rich in meaning and purpose, beyond addiction.

The Journey of Recovery is an Opportunity for Transformation:

It is a chance to reconnect with yourself, your values, and the people you love. It is an opportunity to rewrite your story and build a happier and more authentic future. Believe in your capacity for healing and transformation. You are capable of overcoming pornography addiction and building a more fulfilling and satisfying life.

Remember: You are valuable, loved, and capable of love. Don't give

RODRIGO CIARALO

up on yourself!

CONCLUSION

A Look to the Future and the Path Forward

Throughout this book, we have explored the complex universe of pornography addiction, from its neurobiological foundations to its personal, social, and ethical consequences. We have investigated the effectiveness of Cognitive Behavioral Therapy (CBT) and the importance of integrating therapeutic approaches for complete and lasting recovery. We also discussed the urgent need for effective prevention strategies that promote a culture of sexual health and well-being, grounded in scientific evidence.

Pornography addiction is not an isolated individual problem; it reflects social, cultural, and technological dynamics that shape our understanding of sexuality and relationships (Wright, 2011). The hypersexualization of media, the easy accessibility of online pornography, and the lack of comprehensive sexual education contribute to the normalization of excessive consumption and the increase in addiction cases (Laier et al., 2014).

To combat this problem, a collective effort involving different sectors of society is essential. Governments, educational institutions, families, healthcare professionals, and digital platforms need to join forces to create a safer and healthier environment where sexuality is addressed with respect, responsibility, and awareness (SIECUS, 2023).

The Path Forward: A Multifaceted Approach

- **Invest in Education:** Comprehensive sexual education from childhood is crucial to prevent pornography addiction and promote a healthy view of sexuality (Kirby, 2017). Sexual education programs that promote consent, respect, and effective communication are essential.

- **Strengthen Support:** Expand access to treatment and support services for individuals and families affected by pornography addiction. This includes training mental health professionals in effective approaches for treating pornography addiction.

- **Promote Research:** Encourage scientific research that investigates the causes, consequences, and most effective treatments for pornography addiction. Longitudinal studies and large-scale interventions are needed to evaluate the effectiveness of prevention and treatment strategies.

- **Hold the Industry Accountable:** Demand that the pornographic industry adopts ethical and responsible practices, combating exploitation, abuse, and the production of illegal content. Stricter regulations and monitoring mechanisms are necessary to ensure the protection of vulnerable individuals.

- **Use Technology Consciously:** Develop and utilize technologies that promote sexual health, such as self-monitoring apps, content filters, and online sexual education platforms (Livingston, 2018). Technology can be used both to facilitate access to help resources and to restrict access to harmful content.

- **Foster Dialogue:** Maintain an open and honest dialogue about sexuality and pornography, debunking myths and prejudices. Open communication between parents and children, educators and students, and healthcare professionals and patients is essential to effectively address this sensitive topic.

The future of sexual health and well-being depends on our ability to tackle the challenges of pornography in the digital age. By promoting education, dialogue, accountability, and respect, we can build a society where sexuality is experienced fully, healthily, and consciously.

This book aimed to provide a comprehensive guide on pornography addiction, its consequences, and strategies to combat it.

We hope that the information and reflections presented here contribute to a greater understanding of this complex issue and inspire actions that promote sexual health and the well-being of all.

ABOUT THE AUTHOR

Rodrigo Ciaralo is a dedicated and experienced Brazilian psychologist and neuroscientist, with a career marked by a constant pursuit of knowledge and improvement in the field of mental health. On his website, www.rodrigopsicologia.com, he shares his expertise and offers a variety of resources and services aimed at emotional and psychological well-being.

With a humanized focus and an integrative approach, Rodrigo strives to provide his patients with a welcoming and safe space for personal development and overcoming challenges.

@rodrigociaralo

REFERENCES

Brand, M., Young, K. S., Laier, C., Wéry, A., Pawlikowski, M., & Wegmann, E. (2016). A review of the clinical and treatment characteristics of self-identified "Internet sex addiction". *Sexual Addiction & Compulsivity*, 23(1-2), 124–140.

Cyders, M. A., & Smith, G. T. (2008). Emotion-based dispositions to rash action: Positive and negative urgency. *Psychological Bulletin*, 134(6), 807–843.

Grant, J. E., Potenza, M. N., Weinstein, A., Gorelick, D. A., Hollander, E., & Rounsaville, B. J. (2010). Introduction to behavioral addictions. *The American Journal of Drug and Alcohol Abuse*, 36(5), 233–241.

Kirby, D. (2007). *Emerging Answers 2007: Research findings on programs to reduce teen pregnancy and sexually transmitted diseases.* National Campaign to Prevent Teen and Unplanned Pregnancy.

Koob, G. F., & Volkow, N. D. (2010). Neurocircuitry of addiction. *Neuropsychopharmacology*, 35(1), 217–238.

Laier, C., Pawlikowski, M., Brand, M., Wéry, A., & Young, K. S. (2014). The role of cybersex addiction in the relationship between subjective complaints regarding online sexual activities and psychological distress in a German internet sample. *Cyberpsychology, Behavior, and Social Networking*, 17(12), 794–800.

Livingston, G. (2018). *Unhooked: How young people pursue pleasure, escape pain, and find connection.* Common Sense Media.

SIECUS. (2023). *Sex education: Programs, information, and resources.* Sexuality Information and Education Council of the

United States (SIECUS). https://siecus.org/

Wright, J. H. (2011). *The evolution of desire: Strategies of human mating.* Basic Books.

9 798303 559165